"My Marketing Isn't Working"

How to use strategic marketing to create the business growth you

Susan Banfield & Martin Ellis

ISBN 978-1-326-45842-3

Copyright Susan Banfield & Martin Ellis

The authors have asserted their rights under the Copyright, Designs and Patents Act 1988 to be identified as the authors of this work.

All rights reserved. Without limiting the rights under copyright reserved above, no part of this publication may be reproduced, stored or introduced into a retrieval system or transmitted, in any form or by means (electronic, mechanical, photocopying, recording or otherwise, without the prior written permission of both the copyright owner and the publisher of this book.

Published by: www.b2bgrowth.co.uk

Contents

Introduction 3

Chapter 1 My Marketing Isn't Working - The Problems 4

Chapter 2 MASC™ Strategic Marketing Reviews 11

    The MASC™ Model 12

    Ambition 16

    Strategy 18

    Capability 19

    Strategic Alignment 20

Chapter 3 How Good Is Your Marketing? A Quick Test 22

    Quick Questions - Market 23

    Quick Questions - Ambition 23

    Quick Questions - Strategy 24

    Quick Questions - Capability 24

    Quick Questions - Strategic Alignment 25

Chapter 4 5 Secrets of Marketing Success 26

Chapter 5 Next Steps - Building Strength 39

Introduction

As a Business Owner or Senior Manager in a small to medium sized company (SME) there has never been a more complicated landscape in which your business is trying to grow. Businesses are facing increased competition from non-traditional quarters, markets are rapidly changing, the pace of innovation and growth of digital marketing is huge and keeping pace with customer's needs and expectations is a full time job in itself! This introductory guide is designed to give you an insight into the many benefits of using strategic marketing to support the growth of your business and how to begin to apply this in your business for successful results.

This guide exposes some of the many myths and misconceptions about marketing that frequently underpin the ineffective application of marketing in many businesses, so you can make sure you avoid these traps in your business. We also outline the basic business model we use with companies to help them understand marketing better and the benefit of undertaking Strategic Marketing Reviews which you can use as a template to map out your growth plans.

There are a few simple questions you'll want to look at which will help you to assess how marketing is working for your business currently and to help you identify any areas where further development would be beneficial.

Finally, we suggest a few options you may wish to consider to help you develop your marketing to achieve higher levels of profitable business growth. Here's to your successful growth.

Susan Banfield & Martin Ellis

Chapter 1
My Marketing Isn't Working
- The Problems

Did you know that **"My Marketing Isn't Working"** is the most common reason given by small and medium sized businesses for why they are struggling to achieve higher levels of sustained business growth? But why is that and what are the common underlying problems?

Problem 1: **Limited Marketing Scope.**

Unfortunately, we still find that many companies see marketing as just the promotional and visible aspects: such as what visitors see on your Website, adverts, press releases, emails, flyers, catalogues, exhibition stands, etc. This is rather like focusing on the icing rather than on baking the cake. They don't seem to understand or apply marketing in its wider strategic and organisational role as the underlying way to achieve business goals. If the cake is not properly baked, there is no base for even the prettiest of icing.

Problem 2: **Copying Other Companies.**

Some businesses are often very heavily influenced by what they see and personally like of other companies' promotional activity and then copy it rather than finding their own solution. In business we are not marketing to ourselves, so what we personally like or don't like doesn't really matter. Standing out in the minds of our target customers is what matters. There's even an argument that you should look at what the top people do in your Sector and do something entirely different. If you want to stand out from the crowd, then don't look like everyone else!

Problem 3: **Lack of Customer Input.**

What really matters is what works with your customers, how it satisfies their needs and wants and what they like and don't like. This of course seems obvious, but when was the last time your business sought objective customer feedback about your marketing, or better still

obtained their feedback before you invested in new marketing materials and campaigns? So why would you go blindly forward copying other companies' ideas, when a key part of creating your own unique, and far more effective marketing solution is there for the asking within the heads of your customers? So by either ignoring or by guessing at customer needs, wants and perceptions and by leaving them external to the business, companies become highly vulnerable to changing market conditions and competition through lack of customer insight.

Problem 4: **Not Results Based.**

The problem with copying someone else's ideas is that you don't actually know if the marketing these companies are using, is actually working for them. You can't see behind the scenes of their business. So just because someone else is doing it, it doesn't necessarily mean it is working effectively for them. It certainly doesn't automatically make it the right path for you to follow. Unfortunately many businesses automatically assume it will be working, and therefore believe they should be doing it too.

Problem 5: **Ignorance is Bliss.**

Marketing is not a core skill of most SMEs, so there is a great lack of knowledge about it in many businesses. This ignorance of marketing and of what does and doesn't really work is the root cause of poor sales and profit growth in many businesses. But, instead of educating themselves about marketing and becoming wiser, there is a tendency to carry on doing what they did before and somehow expecting the results to improve. You will never get different results by doing the same things! Ignorance isn't really bliss is it?

Problem 6: **Self-Centred Focus**

A vast amount of B2B marketing promotions activity often looks self-centred. It tends to lack the quality and depth that can only come from a full understanding of customer needs and wants, of competition and of the skilful application of promotional techniques. Far too many businesses focus on providing basic information about their own company, what they do, how they do it and how great they are at it. There is a massive absence of customer empathy and understanding in much B2B marketing, and an underlying false assumption that all customers know what they need or want. Don't forget your marketing should always be focused on your customer and helping them solve their problems and challenges.

Problem 7: **A Marketing Budget with No Purpose**

It's great to have a dedicated marketing budget for your business, but often quite considerable sums of money are spent on 'Marketing', but there is no accountability for that money. Return on investment is not tracked, results of activities like advertising and Pay Per Click are not monitored, it's just a budget figure with no conversion tracking. You get the picture. Marketing Budgets need to be aligned with Marketing Objectives and these need to support business goals. Investment in Marketing, as with all other forms of investment, needs to be monitored for achievement of purpose and the returns it brings to your business so it can continually be fine-tuned and improved.

Problem 8: **Poor Marketing Execution**

Many SMEs are poor at implementing their marketing activity. They email and post out to databases full of incorrect names and addresses, their Websites are out of date, their blogs and news pages are full of old content. They repeat old messages and have nothing new, current or

interesting to say. The content and design of catalogues, brochures, flyers and Websites are produced by 3rd party agencies who themselves aren't usually marketing experts, typically having come from either a design or IT background. These agencies have no real knowledge or understanding about either your business, or your customers.

How Do We Resolve these Problems?

Like an iceberg, 90% of marketing's strength is below the surface, behind the public façade.

It's only when you look under the promotional activity that you will have a true insight into what marketing is really about, what your business should be doing with marketing and what really makes the difference between success and failure.

Marketing is a very broad and specialist business discipline. So here is just a quick flavour of some of the marketing activities that sit under the promotional tip and that you will find behind the scenes of most successful high growth companies.

To be truly effective at marketing there are four key areas you need to develop:

- **Market Knowledge:** you need to nail down your knowledge and understanding of your market, including clarity over your precise market opportunity based on sound market intelligence and a full understanding of your customers' needs, wants, perceptions and expectations and their alternative channels and sources of supply i.e. your competitors.

- **Business Ambitions:** you need absolute clarity of your business's ambitions, goals and objectives in relation to your chosen market opportunity. This needs to include strong market-led leadership in your business and the development of a customer focused culture across the business.

- **Viable Strategies:** you need clarity of both the competitive and optimisation strategies you intend to implement in your business to win that market opportunity. Supported by compelling customer propositions, a clear understanding of your market position and how you intend to defeat your competition. Companies far too often pursue strategies that are inward looking, lack any real competitive advantage, and are often well past their use by date. Marketing plans, budgets and resources either don't exist or are inadequate. You don't want to be one of those.

Marketing Capabilities: what capabilities does your business require to deliver the strategies and actually take the opportunity? What are the products, prices and services, the marketing people, processes, systems and resources needed to meet your ambitions and to fulfil customer expectations? And last but not least, you need to stop taking your lead from what everyone else is doing in your sector in order to make that big move forward.

You need to become your own market-led marketing expert and dig below the superficial level of marketing activity.

Perhaps this quick overview has highlighted some areas where your marketing may not be working as well as you would like. It's time to put a stop to the effects and cost of poor marketing.

So knowing what you now know, perhaps you shouldn't be saying "My Marketing Isn't Working", but instead **"I need to understand marketing much better so I can move my business forward."**

In order to start to better understand how marketing could benefit your business, then your next step should be to have a Strategic Marketing Review. The next chapter looks at this process in more detail.

Chapter 2
MASC™ Strategic Marketing Reviews

MASC™ Strategic Marketing Reviews are a great way to get to the bottom of your marketing challenges and to start to learn and plan how to be able to use marketing more effectively to stimulate and drive growth for your business.

They are an effective new way of auditing, refocusing and revitalising your marketing in order to make it more effective. They cover marketing in its full strategic role, not just in its more obvious promotional one. They enable businesses to see how, by taking a more market & marketing-led approach, they could create a more substantial, sustainable & profitable business.

Strategic Marketing Reviews look beneath the promotional tip of the marketing iceberg, behind the publicly presented façade into what marketing is really about, and at what really makes the difference between success and failure.

So let's take a look at the key elements of a Strategic Marketing Review.

The MASC™ Model

A Strategic Marketing Review is ideally based on an underlying business growth model called MASC™ Strategic Alignment. This simple model ensures that the scope and implications of marketing are reviewed across your whole business.

This MASC™ model covers four key areas as follows:

Market – this covers in detail your company's understanding of its market place and in particular what and where its specific target market opportunities are.

Ambition – this area looks at your company's vision, goals and objectives in relation to the market opportunities you want to take, and to determine if the business is being sufficiently market-led and if your

management and culture are correctly focused on satisfying customer needs and wants.

Strategy – here the Strategic Marketing Review looks at the most misunderstood word in the business dictionary "Strategy" and looks at the plans and approaches your business needs to implement in order to try to achieve the target market opportunity.

Capability – here we review your company's physical, intellectual and financial ability to effectively implement the strategies and take the target market opportunities.

Finally, we will look at **Strategic Alignment** – to see if the four key elements of MASC™ are aligned and working effectively with each other. Interestingly enough, misalignment of the MASC™ elements is a common cause of poor growth, even in companies where individual MASC™ elements appear to be in place and complete. It is a bit like having all the pieces of the jigsaw but not being able to put them together correctly.

Let's look more closely at the four key elements of MASC™ starting with Market.

Market

The vast majority of companies struggling with their marketing will lack a detailed understanding of the market opportunity they are targeting. This is an area in which so many assumptions are often made by companies, that it is only natural that some of their marketing decisions will not work.

Most businesses greatly over estimate their market knowledge and unfortunately a great deal of that knowledge is subjective rather than objective – i.e. it's what they 'think' rather than what they actually know. They tend not to define the value of their own target market

opportunity, but rather think about the whole market or industry trends, which may or may not be that relevant to them.

For example let's say the UK Automotive Supply Chain is valued at around £5.0bn and is growing at 10% per annum according to government statistics. So you might think happy days for everyone in that supply chain. But is that true? There are 2350 UK automotive supply chain companies – are they all growing? Of course not.

Your own market opportunity needs to be defined by a specific target group of customers comprising of those you currently supply and those who you are targeting to supply. By having the knowledge about what they individually and collectively spend and what has and what will happen to them in terms of growth, what % market share you have of this spend and who has the rest, then maybe you are starting to be nearer to understanding your market opportunity.

"The aim of marketing is to know and understand the customer so well the product or service fits him and sells itself." ~ Peter F. Drucker

Ambition

As the saying goes "If you have no idea of where you are going, then any road will take you there!" Unfortunately many businesses lack clarity about where they are trying to get to, especially in terms of connecting their targets to specific qualified market opportunities.

It does make you wonder how much effort is wasted in terms of time and resource due to a lack of clear market driven direction. With different people or departments in their company pulling in different directions all at different paces, they become internally focused on themselves rather than focusing on customers and competitors to achieve a common aim based on a clearly defined market opportunity. The waste in these companies is huge.

Properly understanding and evaluating the market opportunity being targeted by your business will enable you to set clear aims and

objectives, based on the sound knowledge that they are viable and to identify what the best routes are to that market opportunity

Visions, Goals and Objectives set without a market-led focus are often mere wish lists. Business plans or targets, which aren't directly linked to a proven market opportunity are frequently meaningless extrapolations based on past performance, plus a bit for luck! Simply dictating a 20% sales growth next year without any clear knowledge of where it might come from won't help your growth.

> *"It's hard to overcome the pull of conventional wisdom — established ways of doing things, familiar ways to size up markets. That's why it's hard for leaders to do something genuinely new — to embrace one-of-a-kind ideas in a world filled with me-too thinking. But that's the job description for leadership today. After all, if you do things the way everyone else does things, why would you expect to do any better. How are you planning to zig while everyone else zags?"*
>
> \- Bill Taylor

Strategy

Strategies are often termed as being either 'Competitive Strategies' or 'Optimisation Strategies'.

It perhaps goes without saying that Competitive Strategies are those that give you a winning edge with customers. This is usually due to having a unique compelling customer proposition that customers want and your competitors can't match.

Meanwhile Optimisation Strategies are more about developing the day to day activities which you will have in common with your competitors e.g. Quality, Productivity, Efficiency, IT, HR, Finance etc.. Although in the short term advancement in these can give you a competitive edge, in the longer term they probably won't as competitors catch up.

There is a clear distinction between these two types of strategies and you need to know and understand this and to be able to give clear strategic direction accordingly. We see a huge lack of Competitive Strategies and this often explains why many businesses are struggling for growth.

Capability

This is perhaps pretty obvious, but your business does need to have the right products, people, processes, systems, resources, finances and knowledge in order to be able to implement your strategies and to meet

customer needs, wants and demands effectively. It will come as no surprise to you that many businesses fall down on Marketing capability in all these areas. Marketing isn't boxed up into a single person or a department, but it is a way of thinking about and doing business that should pervade your whole company.

Strategic Alignment

It may seem obvious, but all four of these core business elements – Market, Ambition, Strategy and Capability need to align and work effectively with each other. What is commonly found in businesses struggling for growth is that one or more key elements are missing, poorly executed or misaligned.

Misalignment is perhaps the least obvious of these to spot and yet it is the root cause of many growth problems even in well-established large companies. Indeed, as a business grows and becomes older and more established it is more likely to suffer misalignment because of issues such as; complacency, over confidence, a sense of 'entitlement', self-serving functional silos and non-market-led management. These are all quite common conditions leading to strategic misalignment. For example it is not uncommon for a company's ambitions to become

overly focused on shareholder returns or senior management lifestyles which are truly disconnected to the reality of the market place.

You can often see this in FTSE 100 companies, where shareholders push managers for high returns, whilst the company is failing to spot and react to fundamental changes that are taking place in their market place. So don't imagine these issues can't happen to an SME or a young business, because they can and they do.

We have really just scratched the surface of what a Strategic Marketing Review covers, but hopefully you are starting to understand the general direction that a review takes and can begin to map these steps out for your business.

In the next chapter there are a few questions for you, which will start you thinking about Marketing in a different and more strategic way than perhaps you have done before.

Chapter 3
How Good Is Your Marketing?
A Quick Test

Quick Questions - Market

Given the huge importance of objective market intelligence, in order to be able to create the right growth strategies for your target market opportunities, think how would you answer these questions:

MQ1 - What is your current % market share?

MQ2 - What is your forecast for the % growth rate of your target market over the next 3 years?

MQ3 - What is the total £ value of your target market opportunity per annum?

MQ4 - What objective market research do you undertake to evaluate your customer, needs, wants and to forecast demand?

Quick Questions - Ambition

Okay now let's look at your business ambitions, what they are and how they are managed. So what would you say when asked:

AQ1 - Do you have a written Business Growth Plan that outlines your Vision, Goals and Objectives for the coming 3 or more years?

AQ2 - Does that Business Growth Plan include a clear description of your target market opportunities, and the market trends and growth of these?

AQ3- Are your business growth objectives (planned or not) clearly linked to specific market opportunities?

AQ4 - Would you say your business is truly market-led and that all areas of the business are driven by the need to explore then fulfil customer needs, wants and demands?

Quick Questions - Strategy

Now moving on to the dreaded 'S' word 'Strategy'.

SQ1 - Do you have clear strategies written down which direct your team on how you intend to achieve your business growth objectives and challenges?

SQ2 - Do your strategies bear any resemblance to this definition of what a strategy is? (*"A strategy directs and controls a specific course of activity to be taken in order to achieve a stated goal, objective or challenge".*)

SQ3 - Do you have a very clear Competitive Strategy – unique to your business that customers highly value?

SQ4 - If we questioned any one of your management team about what strategy they are working on at this moment in time, would they know?

Quick Questions - Capability

There is little point in having a great market opportunity, the Ambition and the Competitive Strategies if you can't make it happen.

CQ1 - How would you describe marketing in your business: a) something that just 1 or 2 people do, b) something that is at the heart of the business's philosophy and culture and everyone plays their part?

CQ2 - Does your business have a marketing plan and budget, which sets out the next 12 months activities and the purpose of these?

CQ3 - Does your business have within your team a high enough level of strategic marketing knowledge and skills?

CQ4 - What and when were the last three significant market-led innovations made in your business?

Quick Questions - Strategic Alignment

Finally let's take a quick look at a few Strategic Alignment questions; this is where we are looking for a clear connection and synergy between each of the four MASC™ elements with all the other elements. So for example:

SAQ1 - Do you fully research and evaluate market potential and viability before developing or introducing new products or services? (This question is looking to see if your Market Opportunities are aligned with your Strategy & Capability)

SAQ2 - Do the personal likes, dislikes and needs of the business owners and Directors take precedent over the likes, dislikes and needs of customers? (This question is comparing the alignment of your Ambition alignment with your Market Opportunity)

SAQ3 - Does your business operate in functional silos (accounts/operations/sales etc.) that have their own internal focus rather than a shared market and customer focus? (This is questioning if your Capability is aligning with your Market Opportunity)

SAQ4 - Are your strategies based on assumptions due to a limited amount of market intelligence? (This is questioning if your Strategies align with your proven Market Opportunity)

Chapter 4
5 Secrets of Marketing Success

Marketing is a fairly logical, but somewhat complex business discipline. Whilst overall marketing is a fairly robust process, its outcomes are not always 100% possible to tie down. This is because we are always trying to pre-empt and manage the vagaries and idiosyncrasies of dealing with people and their unpredictability.

So, to achieve high levels of business growth through more successful marketing, there is no guaranteed quick fix. The route to marketing success is through considered and sustained application over a prolonged period, although there are many shorter-term benefits along the way. The secret is not to see marketing simply as a task your business has to do, but rather as an overall approach to your on-going business and an underlying tenet or philosophy upon which your business becomes based.

SECRET 1: Become a Market-led Business.

This can be a big ask for many B2B businesses, as so many are often led in other ways, these are the most common:

Technology & Design-Led – the core purpose of the business is to develop new technologies. The business is focused inward on R&D, technical innovation and developing IP – *"build it and they will come"*.

Manufacturing or Operations-Led – the core purpose of the business is to become better at production. The business is focused inward on Reducing Cost, Reducing Time & Improving Quality.

Sales-Led – the core purpose of the business is to sell its existing products or services (what's on the shelf). The business is outward looking but self-centred, focused on making sales and beating competitors.

Profit-Led – the core purpose of the business is to make large profits regardless of how. The business is focused on generating cash and profit.

Visionary-Led – the business is driven to achieve a great purpose or goal, not previously ever attempted or attained by any other business. To solve an unsolved problem, to invent radically new products or solutions or to be fundamentally different in some way.

Competitor-Led – the business takes its lead from other companies and simply seeks to copy and replicate what they do.

Now many of these different business orientations can often be seen to be very successful and some companies are a mix of many. But ultimately all of these approaches would benefit greatly from having an underlying market-led ethos, which is:

Market-Led – the core purpose of the business is to satisfy customer needs, wants and expectations and build mutually beneficial customer relationships. It uses customer, competitor and market intelligence to find (or create) and seize profitable market opportunities. It maintains a detailed knowledge and understanding of;

- the needs, wants, demands, expectations and perceptions of customers
- the strengths and weaknesses of competitors
- the alternative channels and routes to market
- the external influences impacting on the trading environment
- the current and predicted market values and trends

This approach works for one simple reason:

All businesses are dependent on having customers. A Market-Led approach is the best way of finding, winning and keeping them.

So developing a business whose overarching purpose is to create, satisfy and retain customers can be no bad thing. A truly market-led business will also give you a distinct competitive advantage over your competitors.

As David Packard of Hewlett-Packard once famously said, *"Marketing is too important to be left to the marketing people"*. He acknowledged that becoming genuinely market-led isn't that easy, it means listening more than talking. Not something many business bosses are that good at. So management trends and fads over the years have sought to find simpler internally driven alternatives for companies to follow. Business priorities have become directed at finance, IT systems, quality, production, management skills, legal and staffing issues, believing excellence in these to be the new holy grail of creating a great business. But largely these have all failed to achieve the expected results when not aligned to a market-led approach. Designing and manufacturing products better, quicker or cheaper that nobody wants to buy is hardly a route to success. Having skilled managers and staff applying their talents to a declining market, or an uncompetitive customer proposition is also a recipe for failure.

SECRET 2: Invest in Market Intelligence

Those companies who achieve both operational excellence yet remain market-led are the winners and the long-term market leading businesses we see around us. They are those who invest heavily in market research to fully understand customers and competitors. Did you know that the UK market research industry is worth over £3bn per annum and employs 60,000 people? It is larger than both the Music, Film and Newspaper industries combined.

YET – the vast majority of SMEs never use the services of a market research company or undertake routine market research themselves.

The market research industry is on the move and a world away from the old stereotypes of clipboard surveys. The new focus is not on simply gathering 'information' but on UNDERSTANDING customers

and market place dynamics. Businesses who fail to invest in understanding their market run the serious risk of both missing valuable opportunities and making poor decisions based on assumption and guesswork rather than hard evidence.

SECRET 3: Market Opportunity Inspired & Market-led Leadership.

The secret to business success does not come from business bosses staring at their P&L and balance sheet, nor by sitting around tables with their team wondering where the sales went. The task of a business leader is go and find the market opportunity, to find where success lies in the market for their business. Because no one wants to follow a leader if they don't know where they are heading or if they don' have a clear rational for the direction they are taking.

Creating a market-led business isn't always easy, but you can start by inserting some simple questions at every opportunity in your day-to-day conversations with your team and then encourage everyone to do likewise. Some questions to ask in response to planned actions are:

Q1 – *"and what do our customers think of that idea?"*

Q2 – *"and can you show me the market evidence that this will work?"*

Q3 – *"and how does this make us unique and different from competitors?"*

Q4 – *"and are you sure nobody else is already doing this?"*

Q5 – *"and where is the added customer value in that?"*

Q6 – *"how does that translate into customer benefits?"*

Q7 – *"how does that translate into competitive advantage?"*

Q8 – *"and what customer input did you have on that?"*

Q9 – *"and what is the market size and potential for that?"*

Q10 – *"and how are you measuring the customer satisfaction levels of that?"*

SECRET 4: Create Compelling Strategies

To become a good business strategist, you have to be enmeshed in your market place. You have to be inspired by the challenges and opportunities of your customers and by the many conflicts in their minds created by you and your competitors. Your customer propositions need to be clearly differentiated and add value in the eyes of your customers. You'll need to find a uniqueness that you can make your own and that can be protected against copying. Ideally create this uniqueness across the whole business, not just in a product and it will be harder, if not impossible to copy. For example the Virgin Group of companies doesn't just deliver good products and services, but they have inspired customer loyalty and a great affection for the brand and what it stands for.

SECRET 5: Be Highly Competent at Marketing

Great market opportunities, great leaders and great strategies need a great market-led business culture and operational capabilities to support and deliver them. The key areas of marketing expertise you need to have are:

- **Market Research** – so few SMEs invest in market research it's one of the real defining differences between small and large companies. Here is the best opportunity we have to find new opportunities, understand customers and competitors and to make important decisions on facts rather than assumption. Why don't we use it? (*FYI - a common mistake is to assume that sales people are bringing back all*

the market intelligence needed - a big mistake – they don't and they can't). Market research can and should be used to gain intelligence about:

- o Customer needs, wants, expectations
- o Customer demand (volume / value / timings)
- o Customer perceptions
- o Customer satisfaction
- o Customers' customers / end users
- o Industry / Technology trends
- o Channels – distribution & communication
- o Market trends and influences – political, economic, social, technological, legal, environmental.
- o Competitors

"Time spent on market research is time well spent"

- **Innovation Management** – the easiest thing in the world is to continue to do what we have always done. Regardless of how well it works, just plod on doing the same old same old. Innovation is often seen as a risky thing, so *'better the devil we know'*. But in reality any business that stands still is in real terms actually going backwards, and that must ultimately end in grief. There are clearly opportunities to innovate across most if not all areas of your business. Innovation isn't always about reinventing the wheel. Most innovations are simply about updating, enhancing or improving your current processes or products. There are lots of ways you can innovate, but there is one way that is better than all the rest…. **when innovation is customer driven**. You could sit around for weeks thinking about how you could innovate, hold many meetings with your team to discuss it, instigate an 'ideas' box or hold brainstorming sessions. Or you could of course talk to your customers!

- **Product Management** – the products and services we sell or give our customers is a key part of our overall customer proposition. But so many SMEs fail to understand the pros and cons of their offering in the eyes of different customer groups. Learning how you can improve and flex offerings in terms of product specification, add-ons, price, discounting, finance deals, warranty, delivery, distribution channels, packaging, branding and so on. These can all make a big difference – look at the options and test market these with customers and compare and contrast with competitors.

- **Marketing Information Management** – the most valuable thing in your business is what you know about your customers and prospects. Not just the basic details like company name, address, industry sector, size, ownership, etc. but what they buy, when and

how they buy and at what price. Plus key contacts, key decision makers, buying criteria and future potential. These are all essential and highly valuable things for you to know, analyse and use in your business. In addition the recording of incoming communications such as phone calls, emails and mail against customer records. Also the marketing communications sent and responses given, e.g. click throughs from email campaigns, notes of conversations, etc.

These days this information is typically held on a CRM (Customer Relationship Management) System. Many SMEs have these, but most are not used very effectively and quickly become outdated and unloved. It's quite amazing that companies will spend huge energy and investment in new accounts and ERP systems, but CRM systems are nearly always an afterthought bolt on and the poor relation. Yet if your office was burning down and you had to quickly choose between taking a copy of your accounts, or a copy of your customer database with you, which would you choose to save? (*FYI if your answer is a copy of your accounts, then you really are reading the wrong book*). A well set up and effectively used CRM system gives you the opportunity to focus your efforts in the best places and to track the results of both sales and marketing activity. Get one and use it properly.

- **Brand Management** – this isn't just for the big boys. Your brand and your customers' awareness of it, what it stands for, and who and what it's associated with it, can be a hugely powerful influence on customer behaviour and their choice of where and where not to buy. Brand management isn't about sticking your logo on everything, it's about managing what other people know about you, say about you, think about you and how that makes them act. If you think carefully about the brands both small and large with which you personally associate, then you will realise your perception of

these brands will run far more deeply than what their logo looks like.

You will tend to associate brands initially with certain products or services, but then also by what type of people buy them, and where they sit in the market against factors like quality or price. You will also have a view of where they stand relative to their competitors and also if you like or dislike them, or if you would or wouldn't recommend them to someone else. You probably also have a view as to whether they are a successful company, whether they are fair and honest and how well they treat their staff and the sort of people they employ. Quite amazing isn't it that we have this apparent insight (perception) even into companies we don't really know that well? We also know that it is these complex perceptions of companies that ultimately will determine if we would ourselves wish to be associated with them and buy from them. So thinking this through, can you now see just how important managing your own brand really is, and how fully understanding the customer perception of your brand is fundamental to you making the right choices for your business?

- **Marketing Communications** – it had to come, that one thing so many people think marketing is all about – the icing on the cake. Well it's perhaps a little more than that, indeed it's a very important and essential thing to get right (as long as you are doing the others as well). There is no point in finding a great market opportunity, in having inspired leadership, in creating a wonderful market-led business culture able to deliver highly Competitive Strategies and compelling customer propositions if you keep it all under wraps. Just because you are getting it right, doesn't mean the world will automatically beat a path to your door. You need to communicate effectively with your prospects, customers, channel partners,

multipliers, influencers and supporters alike. You need to do this regularly, consistently and professionally, but most importantly you need to be focused on three things:

1) **Your Customers** - making it absolutely clear who you are in business to serve and how your customers benefit from dealing with you.
2) **Your Uniqueness** – the key points of difference and uniqueness of your business and how these add value to your customers and make you a more attractive proposition than your competitors.
3) **Your Brand** - and its positive associations, particularly in terms of associated customers, relative positioning to competitors, and your overall reputation as a supplier.

It's also worth remembering that your customers take a view of your marketing and how well it does or doesn't work for them. Knowing what customers value in terms of your communication and how they like to receive information is just as important as knowing what products and services they might want to buy.

There is no doubt that the most important aspect of marketing communications is............**CONTENT**. Despite what your graphic designer or Web developer may tell you (many of whom have no marketing qualifications), making things look pretty is far less important than what the communication says, and how it says it. That is not to say making things look appealing isn't important, but it must not be done at the expense of not getting the content right (see points 1-3 above).

Another critical factor in effective marketing is **TIMING**. By and large customers are only seriously interested in our marketing communications when they are in the market to buy. If they have just

signed a five year contract with your competitors they are unlikely to be that interested in what you have to say. If you work with customers who work on a fixed term contractual basis, then you may indeed be able to work out key timings. However, for the rest of us we have little choice other than to utilise that great marketing tool….**REPETITION**. The problem with repetition is that it can get pretty boring and customers turn off and unsubscribe. To avoid this we need to think long and hard about content. The skill is to keep your content interesting and engaging, whilst still keeping to the core three areas. By and large customers respond best to content that:

- **Informs** - keeps them informed about their business interests:
    - Their customers (your end users perhaps)
    - Supply chain developments
    - New technologies and innovations
- **Instructs** - them how to do their job better, or quicker or easier or cheaper.
- **Flatters** - makes then look good in the eyes of their competitors, investors or bosses.
- **Compares** - tells them what other customers like them are doing (never underestimate the power of a good case study).
- **Entertains** - they find entertaining or humorous (take great care with humour).
- **Offers** – special deals - because everyone loves a bargain.
- **Trains** - gives them personal development – the chance to learn a new skill or gain useful knowledge.
- **Time Out** - gives them time out of the office (ideally to be treated like royalty.)
- **Gifts** - gives them freebies (within acceptable limits).

So there are plenty of content options to use, just make sure you plan your marketing communications over a sensible period of time giving a

variety of content before you start to repeat the cycle. Ensure you monitor which works best for your customers and use that more frequently.

Content can of course be used in a range of different media types; Websites, brochures, catalogues, flyers, emails, social media, adverts, press releases, telemarketing, exhibitions, videos and so on. Different customers respond better to some content and some media better than others, so don't be a one-club golfer. Make sure your content is available across as many media options as your time and budget allows.

A final word here on 'Digital Marketing'. This really isn't the holy grail of B2B marketing and its initial attraction of being a low cost way of hitting large numbers of customers soon wanes when reality hits home. It is every bit as difficult, if not more so than many more traditional B2B marketing media. However, it is an important part of the overall mix and done well works well. The same rules apply online as do offline i.e. content is King. Whether trying to boost your search engine optimisation, improve your pay per click conversions, getting someone to 'Like' or 'Follow' you, then content is what still counts most. If trying to induce customers to sign up to your e-newsletter, click on your emails or to complete an enquiry form, it is good and relevant content which makes real worthwhile prospects and customers take action.

Chapter 5
Next Steps - Building Strength

Hopefully, you now have a better insight into just some of the many challenges you will face in trying to build strength into your marketing. By following this guide you can begin to refocus and put muscles into your marketing. If you would like some support then there is help at hand and here are just some of your options:

Option 1 – A Strategic Marketing Review.

This comprises a face-to-face meeting at your business with one of our B2B Growth experts to talk through your businesses marketing challenges. This will help you identify some of your underlying marketing issues and look at potential solutions. Typically this meeting will last around 2 hours.

Option 2 – Use B2B Growth coaching services under the UK government's GrowthAccelerator scheme.

This will enable you to have one of our expert coaches working with you over a period of months. This will support not only a more detailed Strategic Review process, but also support your production of a new Strategic Business Growth Plan for your company.

Option 3 – Join our B2B Growth 'Marketing Masters Group'.

This programme combines one to one coaching with on line webinars and workbooks to take you through a Strategic Marketing Review and to support implementation in your business.

Do work through this guide as it will help you to hone your marketing focus on your customers and potential customers. We are here to help you along your way, so please do make contact if we can support you.

Here's to your improved Marketing Journey

If you would like to progress any of the above options or would like to discuss your marketing challenges please contact us.

www.b2bgrowth.co.uk

**Or do call us if you would like to have a conversation
Tel: 01788 474014**

www.ingramcontent.com/pod-product-compliance
Lightning Source LLC
Chambersburg PA
CBHW072304170526
45158CB00003BA/1179